Bolivia

by Cynthia Klingel
and Robert B. Noyed

Content Adviser: Deborah Bender, Ph.D., M.P.H.,
The University of North Carolina

Social Science Adviser: Professor Sherry L. Field,
Department of Curriculum and Instruction, College of Education,
The University of Texas at Austin

Reading Adviser: Dr. Linda D. Labbo,
Department of Reading Education, College of Education,
The University of Georgia

COMPASS POINT BOOKS

Minneapolis, Minnesota

FIRST REPORTS

Compass Point Books
3722 West 50th Street, #115
Minneapolis, MN 55410

Visit Compass Point Books on the Internet at *www.compasspointbooks.com* or e-mail your request
to *custserv@compasspointbooks.com*

Cover: Woman with alpaca on Isla del Sol, Bolivia

Photographs ©: James P. Rowan, cover, 5, 9, 14, 15, 23, 34, 40, 42-43; Trip/F. Good, 4, 33; Trip/J.
Drew, 8; Francis E. Caldwell/Visuals Unlimited, 10-11; Trip/J. Sweeney, 12-13; Hulton
Getty/Archive Photos, 16; Trip/T. Bognar, 18, 19, 28; Trip/M. Barlow, 20, 36; Reuters/David
Mercado/Hulton Getty/ Archive Photos, 22, 39, 41; Trip/M. Jelliffe, 24-25; Trip/N. Price, 26-27;
Trip/P. Musson, 29; AP/Wide World/Sandra Boulanger, 30; Craig Lovell/Corbis, 31; Photo
Network/William Mitchell, 32; D. Cavagnaro/Visuals Unlimited, 37; Photri-Microstock/Lance
Downing, 38; Steve Burke, 45.

Editors: E. Russell Primm, Emily J. Dolbear, and Neal Durando
Photo Researchers: Svetlana Zhurkina and Jo Miller
Photo Selector: Catherine Neitge
Designer: Bradfordesign, Inc.
Cartographer: XNR Productions, Inc.

Library of Congress Cataloging-in-Publication Data
Klingel, Cynthia Fitterer.
    Bolivia / by Cynthia Klingel and Robert Noyed.
        p. cm. — (First reports)
    Includes bibliographical references and index.
    Summary: An overview of the geography, history, people, and social life and customs of the
country of Bolivia, which contains some of the highest mountain peaks in South America.
    ISBN 0-7565-0182-2 (hardcover)
    1. Bolivia—Juvenile literature. [1. Bolivia.] I. Noyed, Robert B. II. Title. III. Series.
    F3308.5 .K55 2002
    984—dc2   2001004371

Table of Contents

"¡Hola!"

▲ *Llamas, members of the camel family, are common in Bolivia.*

"*¡Hola!* Hello! Welcome to Bolivia!" You might hear this greeting if you visit Bolivia.

People have lived in Bolivia for about 10,000

▲ *The Legislative Palace is on Plaza Murillo in La Paz.*

years. Today, many Bolivians still live as people did a long time ago.

Other Bolivians work in the capital cities of La Paz and Sucre. (The government meets in La Paz.

▲ *Map of Bolivia*

The Supreme Court meets in Sucre.) These Bolivians
are educated at colleges. They live much as people in
the United States do.

Most people in Bolivia speak Spanish. Many of them also speak a native language, such as Aymara or Quechua.

Bolivia is a little smaller than the state of Alaska. It covers 424,165 square miles (1,098,587 square kilometers) in South America.

Peru and Chile border Bolivia on the west. Argentina lies to the south. Paraguay touches Bolivia in the southeast. Brazil is on the east and north.

The Andes Mountains in western Bolivia cover half the land. Most people live in the mountains and cities of western Bolivia. Eastern Bolivia is lower and flatter. It has warmer weather.

The head of the government in Bolivia is the president. The people elect the president every five years.

Several times in the past, the military has forced the president to leave. Then a general has taken over the country. Today, however, Bolivia has an elected government.

Mountains and Valleys

▲ *Poyachatas Volcano is part of the Andes Mountains area.*

You can see the beautiful Andes Mountains in Bolivia. Some of the highest peaks in South America are in Bolivia.

The snowy peak of Mount Illimani is one of the most visible landmarks in La Paz. It is 21,000 feet (6,405 meters) high. Some parts of the country are very cold while others have **tropical** rain forests.

The second-largest lake in South America is Lake Titicaca. It is on the border between Bolivia and Peru. A high **plateau** called the Altiplano lies between

▲ *The Altiplano lies between two mountain ranges.*

▲ *The village of San Pedro is in the Yungas.*

two mountain ranges in the Andes. Most Bolivians live in this part of the country. It is one of the highest places where people live in the world.

The Altiplano is always cool, between 40 and 55 degrees Fahrenheit (4 and 13 degrees Celsius). Some parts of the Altiplano are much colder, however.

The plants that grow on the Altiplano can live at high elevations. One of these, quinoa, is a very healthy grain. It is often used in tasty soups.

A part of Bolivia called the Yungas lies on the eastern side of the Andes. This area has high peaks and low valleys.

Many Bolivian people live in the

▲ *During the rainy season, the Chaco is one of the hottest places in South America.*

valleys. Half of the farmland in Bolivia is in this area. Some people say that it always feels like springtime in the Yungas.

In eastern Bolivia, the land is lower and flatter. The northern lowlands are covered with swamps and tropical rain forests. The rain forests have hundreds of kinds of trees and plants.

In the southern lowlands of Bolivia, an area called the Chaco is a dry desert most of the year. But in the rainy season, so much water falls that the Chaco becomes a swamp. During the rainy season, the Chaco is one of the hottest places in South America.

History of Bolivia

▲ *Huge carvings at the Tiahuanaco ruins were made more than 1,000 years ago.*

Bolivia has a long history. People settled in Bolivia thousands of years ago.

In the 1400s, the Inca took over what is now western Bolivia. The Inca were powerful people with many skills. They knew how to build roads, bridges, and great cities. They spoke a language called Quechua. Many Bolivians still speak this language.

The Inca ruled for many years. At first, they were very strong. Then they began to fight with one another. They grew weaker.

In 1531, soldiers came from Spain. The Spanish soldiers took the land. They made slaves of the Inca.

The Spanish ruled Bolivia for several centuries. In the 1770s, the native people began to fight

◀ *A statue in La Paz of General Simón Bolívar, after whom Bolivia is named*

▲ Bolivian soldiers march through a fort they built during the Chaco War.

against the harsh rule of the Spanish. Wars raged between the Bolivians and the Spanish people. It was a hard time for the country. Bolivia defeated Spanish forces in 1825. Spanish rule in Bolivia was over.

The country was named after General Símon Bolívar from Venezuela. He led the fight for independence in many South American countries.

Bolivia went to war against Paraguay in 1932. Thousands of Bolivians were killed. Many more were hurt. This war is called the Chaco War.

In 1960, a **revolutionary** from Argentina named Che Guevara led a fight against the military government of Bolivia. For awhile he was successful in trying to change the government. The army killed him in 1967.

Over the past seventy years, Bolivia has dealt with many changes in its government. The country has had many presidents and leaders. Some of them took power by force. Recently, presidents have been elected.

People of Bolivia

▲ *A native woman with a baby leads a llama on Isla del Sol on Lake Titicaca.*

More than half of the people in Bolivia are related to the Quechua and the Aymara. These native peoples lived in the area before the arrival of Europeans.

Sometimes these people are called Amerindians. They are also called **campesinos**, which means "people who work the land."

There are smaller groups of Guarani

▲ *Most Bolivians related to the Spanish live and work in cities, such as La Paz.*

and Chipaya people. Each group has its own customs and traditions.

A small number of Bolivians trace their relatives to Europe. They are very proud of their past and proud

▲ *Children from Coroico in the Yungas*

to be Bolivians. Throughout Bolivia's history, these Bolivians have also contributed greatly to the country's culture.

About one-third of Bolivians are European and native Indian. They are called **mestizos**.

Mestizos speak Spanish. Many also speak Quechua or Aymara. Many of these Bolivians produce traditional Bolivian art.

Another group of Bolivians is the Afro-Bolivians. In the 1500s, the Spanish discovered silver in Bolivia. They brought slaves from Africa to work in the mines.

The Afro-Bolivian slaves were also forced to work in the fields and homes of wealthy people. They had to work very hard and their masters often beat them. Slavery was completely outlawed in 1851.

Today the Afro-Bolivians are still not always treated well. Their special type of music, called *saya*, however, is now becoming popular.

▲ *A member of a saya group performs during a carnival in Oruro.*

Over the past sixty years, people have come from different countries to live in Bolivia. People have come from Poland, Germany, and Japan. They are bringing new cultures to the country. Bolivia has many races and cultures today.

A Harsh Land

▲ *Lake Titicaca is on the border between Bolivia and Peru.*

Bolivia is one of the poorest countries in South America. It has many **natural resources** that are not yet developed.

A system of roads connects the major cities. The roads to small towns and country areas are not good.

▲ Miners in the shaft of a tin mine in Potosi

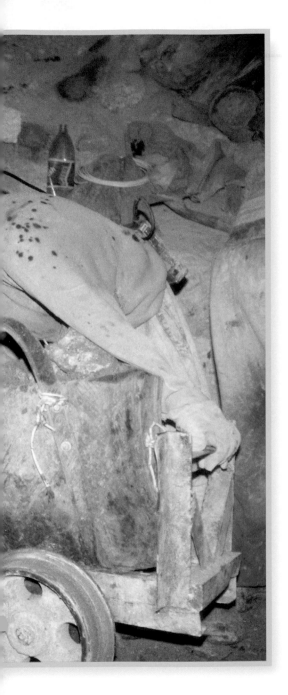

It is also difficult to travel over the mountains.

Mining is an important part of the economy in Bolivia. It is not easy because the work is dangerous.

In the past, Bolivia produced lots of tin. Today the country mines tin, silver, gold, lead, iron, nickel, and other minerals.

Bolivia also produces oil and natural gas. People first found oil in Bolivia in the 1890s.

Today Bolivia produces oil for itself and sells oil to other countries, too. Bolivia also

▲ *Cattle are herded along a rural road near Santa Cruz.*

sells natural gas to Argentina, Brazil, and Chile.

Many Bolivians are farmers. Some grow fruits and vegetables. Others grow coffee and raise cattle.

In many places, the soil is not good for farming. Farmers are trying to develop grains that can grow at high elevations. Barley and quinoa are such grains.

Alpacas and vicuñas are also raised in the mountains. These animals are related to camels. They have wool that is valuable. People make beautiful yarn from it.

Music in the Villages

▲ *A traditional dancer performs at a folk club in La Paz.*

Bolivians love to dance and make music. In La Paz, a school called the National Academy of Fine Arts educates many students. They come here to study music, painting, sculpture, and ceramics.

The music in Bolivia is simple and beautiful. Young Bolivian boys spend hours each day watching over their

▲ *Children playing panpipes*

animals in the field. To pass the time, the boys often play traditional instruments such as the *zampoña*. This is a flute made of reed tubes. Other boys learn to play the guitar or drums.

Most young men grow up playing an instrument. Bands of these young men play in the villages.

▲ *A man plays in honor of the rising sun during an Aymara new year celebration.*

People from the Altiplano play music that sounds sad. People from the Chaco, however, play music that is lively. In the past, Bolivian musicians played their instruments but did not sing. Today, Bolivian people have started to add words to their songs.

▲ *A churrango, which is made from the shell of an armadillo, sounds like a guitar.*

Bolivian musicians play several kinds of instruments. They use flutes made of reeds. They also play drums, cow horns, and violins or fiddles.

An instrument called the *churrango* is made from the shell of an **armadillo**. It is small and sounds like a guitar. At celebrations, people like to dance.

Bolivian people weave beautiful clothing and blankets. The colorful materials they weave are smooth and strong. They weave wool from sheep, llamas, or alpacas in special Bolivian patterns and styles. In one style, red and black are woven side by side. Bolivian weavers are highly skilled.

▲ *An Aymara weaves a beautiful cloth.*

Ponchos and Braids

▲ *Many Bolivian women wear brightly colored clothes and bowler hats.*

In the cities of Bolivia, people dress like people in the United States. But on farms and in other parts of Bolivia, people may still wear traditional clothes, especially on holidays.

The women and girls who dress traditionally wear brightly colored clothes. When it is cold, they wear several skirts on top of one another to keep warm. They put bright shawls around their shoulders. They wear their long hair in braids. Bolivian women often wear bowler hats.

Bolivian men wear ponchos, shirts, and pants. A poncho is a cloak that looks like a blanket with holes for the head and arms. The men often wear a cap with earflaps.

Traditionally, clothes were woven from wool by hand. Today, most clothes are made in small factories, but the styles are the same.

◄ An Aymara in traditional clothing works on a reed boat.

Eating in Bolivia

▲ *A woman buys tomatoes at a street market in La Paz.*

In Bolivia, people eat many different kinds of foods. The main part of the meal is often meat with potatoes or rice.

Potatoes are popular in Bolivia. Farmers grow many kinds of potatoes—white, red, yellow, and purple! Bolivians also eat other vegetables with their meals.

In the tropical areas of Bolivia, people grow many wonderful fruits. They grow oranges, tangerines, papaya, mango, and guava.

For hundreds of years, Bolivian people have grown and eaten quinoa and oca. Quinoa is a plant with a heavy head of seeds that are roasted and boiled to make porridge. Quinoa tastes a little like nuts.

Oca is a long, thin root vegetable. It can be eaten plain or mixed with other foods.

▲ *Colorful oca is a root vegetable.*

Fiestas

Bolivians love to celebrate. In Bolivia, a celebration is called a **fiesta**. Some villages have a fiesta almost every week!

▲ *Girls perform a traditional dance at a celebration near Lake Titicaca.*

▲ Bolivia's biggest festival is Carnival, where thousands of people take part in parades.

Bolivians wear their best clothes at fiestas. Sometimes they wear handmade costumes and masks.

The biggest fiesta in Bolivia is called the Carnival, or *La Diablada Carnival*. The Carnival is held once a year about six weeks before Easter. For several days, Bolivians march in parades, play music, and dance in the streets.

Religion in Bolivia

▲ *The Roman Catholic church in Copacabana was built in the seventeenth century.*

Almost all Bolivians are Roman Catholic. Native
Bolivians who live outside the cities still follow many
of the old beliefs. Some of these are hundreds of
years old.

Some native Bolivians believe in *Pachamama*, or

the "Earth Mother." She protects the people, animals, and plants.

Some Bolivians believe in traditional medicine. A witch doctor is called a *yatiri*. People go to the yatiri with their problems.

People also go to a wise man called an *amauto*. A long time ago, the amauto would remember everything people needed to know. When people needed information, they asked the amauto questions.

▲ *An Aymara witch doctor makes an offering on the shores of Lake Titicaca to Pachamama, the Earth Mother.*

Bolivia Today

Bolivia has a long and fascinating history. It is a fun, safe, and interesting place to visit.

People come to learn about the traditions and to climb the beautiful mountains. Bolivians are proud of their country, their traditions, and their history.

If you visit Bolivia, you will learn more about this ancient land. When you leave, you may say, "*Gracias!* Thank you! I enjoyed my visit to Bolivia."

◄ *Huayna Potosi Mountain in Condoriri National Park*

Glossary

armadillo—a mammal covered by hard, bony plates

campesinos—another word for Amerindians, meaning "people who work the land"

fiesta—a holiday or festival

mestizos—people who are European and native Bolivian

natural resources—minerals, forests, or water

plateau—high, flat ground

revolutionary—someone involved in fighting against a government

tropical—hot and rainy

Did You Know?

- Most historians believe that Butch Cassidy and the Sundance Kid died in a shoot-out with Bolivian soldiers in 1908. The famous outlaws were on the run after robbing a mining company payroll wagon. Their gang was called the Wild Bunch.

- In Bolivia, the most popular sport is soccer.

- Tinku is a traditional Bolivian sport. It starts as a dance and ends as a fistfight.

At a Glance

Official name: Republic of Bolivia

Capital: La Paz (legislative); Sucre (judicial)

Official languages: Spanish, Quechua, Aymara

National song: "Himno Nacional" ("National Anthem")

Area: 424,165 square miles (1,098,587 square kilometers)

Highest point: Nevado Sajama, 21,463 feet (6,546 meters) above sea level

Lowest point: Rio Paraguay, 295 feet (90 meters) below sea level

Population: 8,329,100 (2000 estimate)

Head of government: President

Money: Boliviano

Important Dates

1400s	The Inca arrive in Bolivia and take control.
1531	Spanish soldiers arrive in Bolivia and take control.
1550s	The Spanish discover silver in Bolivia.
1825	Bolivia declares its independence from Spain.
1879–1883	Bolivia fights in the War of the Pacific.
1932–1935	Bolivia fights in the Chaco War.
1952	Military rulers are overthrown and a president is elected.
1980s	Rule by the people is established in Bolivia.
1995	Bolivia begins selling state-owned businesses to private companies.

At the Library

Hermes, Jules. *The Children of Bolivia*. Minneapolis: Carolrhoda Books, 1996.

Jacobsen, Karen. *Bolivia*. Chicago: Childrens Press, 1991.

Pateman, Robert. *Bolivia*. New York: Marshall Cavendish, 1996.

On the Web

Factmonster Almanac

http://www.factmonster.com/ipka/A0107345.html

For more information about the geography and history of Bolivia

Wild Treasures of Bolivia

http://animal.discovery.com/exp/bolivia/bolivia.html

For games and information about the animals of Bolivia

Through the Mail

Quipus—Bolivia Cultural Council, Inc.

P.O. Box 6297

Yorkville Station

New York, NY 10128

To get more information about the culture and life of Bolivians today

On the Road

Museum of Latin American Art

628 Alamitos Avenue

Long Beach, CA 90802

413/458-2303

To see exhibits featuring Bolivian and other South American art

About the Authors

Cynthia Klingel has worked as a high school English teacher and an elementary school teacher. She is currently the curriculum director for a Minnesota school district. Cynthia Klingel lives with her family in Mankato, Minnesota.

Robert B. Noyed started his career as a newspaper reporter. Since then, he has worked in school communications and public relations at the state and national level. Robert B. Noyed lives with his family in Brooklyn Center, Minnesota.